MW01128174

How to Play the Otamatone for Beginners

The Ultimate Guide to Learning, Playing, and Becoming Proficient at the Instrument

Table of Contents

Introduction

Do you have the desire to create unique, whimsical, and utterly enchanting music? Perhaps you've dreamed of an instrument that defies convention, blends innovation with entertainment, and sparks joy with every note. If you're nodding in agreement, then "How to Play the Otamatone" is about to become your new best friend.

This book isn't merely another guide to playing an instrument. It's your portal to a world of musical magic, wrapped in simplicity and designed with beginners in mind. If you've ever hesitated to pick up a musical instrument, been intimidated by complex theory or intricate techniques, or simply crave a creative outlet that's as joyful as it is melodious, this book is your ticket to a musical adventure.

What Sets This Book Apart

You might wonder what makes "How to Play the Otamatone" stand out amid a sea of similar titles. Here are a few things that set this book apart:

- **Elegantly Easy to Understand:** The art of playing the Otamatone has been distilled into crystal-clear, jargon-free language, making even the most complex concepts a breeze to grasp. Regardless of prior musical experience, you'll find this book a friend, not a daunting tutor.

- **Perfect for Beginners:** Are you a novice in the world of music? Fear not. "How to Play the Otamatone" is tailored to beginners and will guide you gently, starting from the basics to advanced techniques.

- **Hands-on Methods and Instructions:** Learning by doing is the best way to master any skill. This book follows this method. You'll find practical, hands-on instructions that will have you playing the Otamatone in no time.

- **Unleash Your Creative Spirit:** This book isn't about teaching you how to play an instrument. It's about igniting your creativity. You'll find inspiration on every page and discover how to infuse melodies with your unique personality and style. Whether you want to create soothing lullabies or catchy tunes, you'll have all the tools to craft them.

- **A Journey of Joy:** Playing the Otamatone is not only about making music but also about having fun. The joy that comes from creating music with this instrument is infectious, and this book is your guide to embracing every moment of your musical adventure.

When you open "How to Play the Otamatone," you embark on a remarkable journey. You'll explore the history and charm of this unique instrument, discover the ins and outs of its delightful sound, and learn how to perform your favorite songs while improving your skills in a simple, fun, and engaging way.

By the end, you won't only be playing the Otamatone. You'll be creating remarkable music. You'll become lost in whimsy and innovation, delighting yourself and those fortunate enough to listen.

Whether you're an absolute beginner or a seasoned musician looking to add something extraordinary to your repertoire, "How to Play the Otamatone" will empower you with the knowledge and confidence to turn your musical dreams into stunning realities.

Chapter 1: Background to the Otamatone

The Otamatone, a musical wonder resembling a delightful crossbreed between a tadpole and a musical note, holds a unique and captivating charm that can't be ignored. This chapter delves into the captivating background of the Otamatone, unravels its whimsical nature, and explores its significance in music and creative expression. Whether you're a complete novice in the realm of music or an experienced musician looking for a new adventure, this chapter covers it all.

1. The Otamatone is a musical wonder. Source: TheFakeSullyG, CC BY-SA 4.0 <https://creativecommons.org/licenses/by-sa/4.0>, via Wikimedia Commons: https://commons.wikimedia.org/wiki/File:TheRealSullyG_Otamat ones.jpg

Exploring the Unique and Whimsical Nature of the Otamatone

The Otamatone's charm goes beyond its distinctive design, and several aspects make it truly unique and whimsical:

The Quirky Appearance

The sight of an Otamatone is nothing short of a visual delight. It has a slender stem as its body, topped with a round musical note for a head. This musical note, painted with a wide smile, gives the instrument an enchanting face that never fails to make you smile. It's as if the Otamatone is inviting you to embark on a musical adventure. This unique design blurs the line between art and technology, resulting in a charming instrument that's as captivating as it is innovative.

The Playful Side of Music

More often than not, music is associated with seriousness and formality. However, the Otamatone turns this stereotype on its head. It embodies the playful spirit of music, encouraging you to explore your musical creativity with unbridled joy. It's about playing notes and embracing the pure delight of making music. This feature makes the Otamatone perfect for children and adults, ensuring music remains a joyful and entertaining experience.

Interactivity Redefined

Unlike traditional instruments where you pluck strings or press keys, the Otamatone offers a tactile and visual experience. Your fingers dance along its stem, creating a harmonious connection between you and the music you produce. This hands-on approach turns every session into a mesmerizing performance, inviting you to express yourself with playful gestures.

Expressive Facial Gestures

The Otamatone isn't just an instrument. It's a character with a personality. Its enchanting face, painted with a wide smile and expressive eyes, can mimic human-like emotions. When you play it, you create music and convey feelings through a captivating visual spectacle. Its cheerful nature will match your joy or reflect your mellow melodies, adding an extra layer of expressiveness to your music.

Both a Musical Gadget and a Conversation Piece

While most musical instruments are meant for serious practice and performance, the Otamatone doubles as a musical gadget and a conversation starter. Its innovative and playful design makes it a source of amusement and a musical instrument. Place it on your desk, and it becomes a talking point, drawing curious glances and sparking conversations.

Sound Synthesis Meets Creativity

The Otamatone's sound is a product of sound synthesis technology. It allows you to explore electronic tones that are remarkably versatile. The sliding of your fingers along the stem translates into a shift in pitch. This unique quality provides a plethora of creative opportunities. You will craft melodies that seem otherworldly, or you can aim for soothing tunes wrapping around your senses like a comforting blanket.

Portable Whimsy

One of the best features of the Otamatone is its portability. It's a pocket-sized musical companion you can take wherever you go. Whether at a park, on a picnic, or relaxing in your backyard, the Otamatone is always there to serenade you with its melodious tunes.

A World of Accessories

The Otamatone has a host of whimsical accessories. From adorable plushie covers transforming it into a lovable creature to miniature Otamatones fitting in the palm of your hand, the accessories make the whole experience even more charming. They allow you to personalize your Otamatone, adding a touch of individuality to your musical journey.

Understanding Its Role in Music and Creative Expression

To truly grasp the significance of the Otamatone, you must explore its role in music and creative expression.

Unbridled Musical Versatility

The Otamatone doesn't pigeonhole you into a single genre or style. It's a versatile instrument that will be your voice in an array of musical genres, from classical symphonies to contemporary pop hits. This versatility empowers you to craft melodies uniquely yours, pushing the boundaries of what's possible.

Creativity Unleashed

The Otamatone is an endless source of creative inspiration. Its unconventional design and unique sound are a wellspring of creativity. Do you want to replicate the melodious chirping of a bird? The Otamatone has your back. How about recreating the iconic tunes of classic video games? It will effortlessly appease you. It encourages you to think outside the box, giving your musical expression a distinct edge.

A Conversation Starter

The Otamatone is a social catalyst. Whip it out at a social gathering, and you're bound to spark curiosity. It's a fantastic icebreaker setting the stage for engaging conversations and forging new connections. With the Otamatone in your hand, your gatherings will never be the same again. They'll be filled with laughter and musical interludes lingering in your memory.

Embracing Expressiveness

What sets the Otamatone apart is its unique ability to convey emotions through music. The sliding motion of your fingers along its stem enables you to produce expressive and dynamic changes in pitch. You can mimic laughter, tears, excitement, or any emotion with your music. You will tell a story through your music, evoking feelings and connecting with your audience profoundly.

Collaborative and Engaging

The Otamatone isn't only a solo act but also a fantastic instrument for collaboration. It naturally attracts attention, making it a hit at parties, gatherings, and musical meetups. You will easily harmonize with other musicians and add a unique flavor to group performances. Its unconventional appearance and sound often draw in other musicians, turning your sessions into memorable creative exchanges.

A Gateway to Music Education

For educators and parents, the Otamatone is an excellent tool to introduce children to music. Its intuitive design makes it accessible to kids as young as six years old. It's a stepping stone into the world of melody and rhythm, sparking an early interest in music. Additionally, its playful appearance makes learning enjoyable.

A Digital Playground

The Otamatone is not bound by physical constraints thanks to its electronic nature. To explore digital music creation, you can connect it to various devices, like smartphones, tablets, or computers. With the right apps and software, you can produce a wide range of sounds, opening the door to electronic music production and sound design. It's your gateway to an entire digital music playground.

Setting Expectations for Beginners

Now that you know about the whimsical charm and creative potential of the Otamatone, it's time to set your expectations as a beginner and prepare for the exciting journey ahead.

No Prior Musical Experience Required

Perhaps one of the most remarkable aspects of the Otamatone is its accessibility. You don't need prior musical knowledge or experience. If you've never plucked a string or pressed a key on a musical instrument before, the Otamatone is the ideal introduction to music.

Step-by-Step Guidance

This book is your trusty companion, designed with beginners in mind. You'll find clear and easy-to-follow step-by-step instructions. Whether you're a first-time musician or looking to diversify your repertoire, you'll progress steadily and confidently with the help of the following chapters. Each chapter is crafted with precision, ensuring you're equipped with the necessary knowledge and skills to make your Otamatone journey smooth and enjoyable.

The Joy of Learning

Like with any instrument, playing the Otamatone isn't only about reaching a destination. It's about relishing every step of the journey. You'll experience the sheer joy of creating music from the beginning, which intensifies as you become more proficient. With each new skill you master, you'll be smiling, laughing, and utterly immersed in the enchanting world of the Otamatone. It's a journey filled with moments of discovery, creativity, and, above all, a deep love for music.

A Musical Adventure Awaits

As a beginner, you're about to embark on a musical adventure that's fun and rewarding. The Otamatone is your trusty steed, and this book is your treasure map. It's a journey that leads to your musical potential discovery. Whether you dream of playing catchy pop tunes, serene classical compositions, or crafting unique melodies, the Otamatone will be your faithful companion every step of the way.

Connecting with a Community

The Otamatone community is a vibrant and welcoming group of musicians who share your passion for this enchanting instrument. As you progress, you'll connect with fellow enthusiasts, share your experiences, and learn from others.

Embrace the Fun

Above all, remember the journey of learning to play the Otamatone is meant to be enjoyable. The instrument's whimsical nature and unique sound ensure every practice session is infused with laughter and amusement. So, embrace the fun, relish the learning process, and savor the joy that comes from creating music.

With your Otamatone in hand, your curiosity ignited, and the knowledge and guidance of this book, you're fully prepared to set off on a musical adventure promising joy, creativity, and unforgettable moments. The chapters ahead are your gateway to becoming a master of whimsical melodies and discovering the incredible Otamatone. Get ready to play, create, and be enchanted by this remarkable instrument. Your symphonic adventure starts now.

Chapter 2: Unboxing and Understanding Your Otamatone

Unboxing your Otamatone is akin to unwrapping a box of pure musical joy. As you peel back the packaging, you'll find a tadpole-like object with a musical note head begging to be your musical companion. The magic starts when you snap the head onto the stem with a satisfying click, like two old friends reuniting. With fresh batteries tucked inside, it's ready to unleash its quirky electronic melodies, bringing a smile to your face with every press and slide of your fingers.

In this chapter, you'll unbox and explore the fascinating intricacies of this unique musical instrument.

Overview of the Otamatone's Features and Components

It's time to begin by exploring the different features and components that make this instrument a visual and auditory delight.

2. The Otamatone's body is where the music comes to life. Source: Alexander Krasnov, CC BY-SA 4.0 <https://creativecommons.org/licenses/by-sa/4.0>, via Wikimedia Commons: https://commons.wikimedia.org/wiki/File:%D0%96%D0%B0%D0%BB%D0%B5%D0%B9%D0%BA%D0%B0-%D0%BB%D0%BE%D0%B6%D0%BA%D0%B0!_%D0%A4%D0%BE%D0%BB%D0%BA-%D1%88%D0%BE%D1%83_%D0%B3%D1%80%D1%83%D0%BF%D0%BF%D0%B0_%D0%9A%D0%BE%D0%BB%D1%8F%D0%B4%D0%BA%D0%B8_(%D0%90%D0%BD%D1%81%D0%B0%D0%BC%D0%B1%D0%BB%D1%8C_%D0%BD%D0%B0%D1%80%D0%BE%D0%B4%D0%BD%D0%BE%D0%B9_%D0%BC%D1%83%D0%B7%D1%8B%D0%BA%D0%B8_%D0%9A%D0%BE%D0%BB%D1%8F%D0%B4%D0%BA%D0%B8).jpg

1. **The Body:** The Otamatone's body is where the music comes to life. Nestled inside this slender stem are the electronic components producing its distinctive sound. It usually houses AA or AAA batteries that power the instrument.

2. **The Head:** At the bottom of the stem is the Otamatone's head. It's an integral part of the

instrument's design, resembling a round musical note with a wide smile. The head adds a touch of personality and whimsy to the Otamatone, making it feel like a musical companion instead of just another instrument. However, the head is not only for show. It houses essential components, creating the charming sounds the Otamatone is known for.

3. **The Stem Switch:** The heart of the Otamatone lies in its stem switch. It's where you bring the instrument to life, crafting melodies and experimenting with sounds. The stem switch comprises a rubber strip on the stem. You control the pitch by pressing or sliding your fingers along this strip, producing a wide range of electronic tones.

4. **The Speaker:** You'll find the Otamatone's speaker just below the head. It's where the music you create is amplified and shared with the world. As you play your melodies, the speaker reproduces the sounds you generate, allowing you to share your music and joy with those around you.

5. **The Power Switch and Volume Control**: The Otamatone has a power switch and a volume control on the back of the stem. The power switch is where you turn it on and off. When not in use, switch it off to conserve battery life. As the name implies, the volume control allows you to adjust the volume. This feature is particularly useful when playing in different settings or around other people.

Proper Assembly and Care

Now that you've unpacked your Otamatone, it's time to ensure it's in optimal condition. Here's a walkthrough of assembling your Otamatone, tips on care and maintenance, and guidance on keeping it in the best shape possible.

Assembly: Bringing Your Otamatone to Life

Are you ready to create your musical friend? Most Otamatones come in two parts: the main body and the head. Here's how to put the pieces together and bring your musical companion to life:

1. **Unwrapping**: When your Otamatone arrives, treat it like the treasure it is. Gently unwrap it from its packaging, as delicate as you would with a fragile toy. Take a moment to appreciate its uniqueness, from its quirky design to its charming face.

2. **Face the Music**: The head of your Otamatone usually boasts a cute smile or a delightful animal face. Now, align it with the hole at the top of the main body. Make sure it's centered and its 'mouth' is pointing up. The alignment is for aesthetics and proper functionality. When the head is correctly positioned, your Otamatone will produce the characteristic quirky sounds it's known for.

3. **Firm but Friendly:** Gently but firmly press the head onto the main body. You should feel it lock into place without the need to force it. Remember, the key here is a gentle touch. You don't want to twist or bend anything.

4. **Eye on the Prize:** Double-check the alignment. The eyes (if your Otamatone has them) should be level. If things look a bit wonky, don't worry. Just give it a little nudge until it sits right. Proper alignment will help press the keys accurately, producing the desired tones.

5. **Key Testing, Music Quest:** Before diving in, give the keys a friendly press to ensure they work. If any seem a bit shy or stuck, take a peek for obstructions or misalignment.

6. **Cherish the Quirks**: Finally, take a moment to cherish the quirks and charms of your Otamatone's design. This instrument is a conversation starter, a mood-lifter, and your partner in musical mischief.

Proper assembly isn't only about functionality. It's about giving your new musical friend a warm welcome to your world. Following these simple assembly steps with care and a sprinkle of joy, you're ready to make music with your Otamatone and have a whimsical time together.

Care and Maintenance: Keeping Your Otamatone Happy

Proper care and maintenance are vital to keep your Otamatone in good working condition. Here are essential tips to keep your quirky, musical buddy in top shape:

1. **Clean the Surface**: Your Otamatone will get a little dusty from time to time, especially if it's been busy playing catchy tunes. Grab a soft, lint-free cloth and give it a gentle wipe-down. This gentle

cleaning maintains the visual appeal of your Otamatone and ensures dust or debris does not interfere with the keys or the rubber strip.

2. **Handle with Care**: The Otamatone's head, while designed to be whimsical and expressive, is also fragile. Twisting or pushing too hard on the head will lead to a not-so-happy Otamatone. Hold it by the main body or use the strap if available when handling it. It prevents undue pressure on the head and keeps it in its best condition.

3. **Store Safely:** After a long day of music-making, your Otamatone deserves a comfy resting place. Store it in a cool, dry spot away from extreme temperatures, sunlight, or moisture.

4. **Protect the Rubber Strip:** That rubber strip on your Otamatone is like its vocal cords. Keep it clean by avoiding using dirty or oily fingers. If it gets a little messy, a gentle wipe-down with a damp cloth will do the trick. You want those notes to come out clear and crisp.

5. **Battery Maintenance**: If your Otamatone runs on batteries, don't forget to change them. Leaving in old batteries leads to battery corrosion. Also, consider using rechargeable batteries, an eco-friendly and budget-friendly choice.

6. **Keep It Dry:** If you accidentally spill something on it, disconnect the battery and let it dry completely.

7. **Check for Loose Screws:** The Otamatone's screws sometimes get a bit loose from all that

groovy music. Tighten them gently when necessary.

8. **Use a Strap:** If your Otamatone has strap hooks, consider giving it a stylish accessory. A strap allows a comfortable playing experience and prevents accidental drops or damage.

9. **Seek Professional Repairs**: If your Otamatone experiences issues you cannot resolve, seek professional repairs. Attempting to fix complex problems yourself can lead to further damage. Someone qualified will diagnose and cure any issues.

By following these care and maintenance tips, you'll have a happy, healthy Otamatone that's always ready to play and spread joy. So, go ahead, give your Otamatone the love and care it deserves, and keep the music flowing.

Getting Familiar with the Otamatone's Interface and Controls

Now that your Otamatone is assembled and ready to go, it's time to dive into its interface and controls. Understanding these aspects will help you make the most of your musical journey.

- **The Note Selector:** At the top of the Otamatone's head, you'll find a musical note with small dots or lines. These markings represent different musical notes. To change the pitch and produce various sounds, you only need to slide your finger up or down the stem, stopping at the desired note. This feature allows you to play melodies in different octaves, adding depth and diversity to your performances.

- **Producing Sound:** The true magic of the Otamatone happens at its mouth interface. It's where you create sound. Pressing or sliding your fingers along the rubber strip changes the pitch and produces many electronic tones. The sliding motion is akin to a vocalist altering their pitch, giving your melodies a vocal-like quality. Experiment with different finger placements and movements to explore the full spectrum of sounds you can produce.

- **Embrace the Learning Curve:** As you learn to play the Otamatone, you may encounter a learning curve, especially if you're new to music. Don't be discouraged if it takes practice to achieve your desired sound. The Otamatone rewards experimentation. Start with simple tunes and familiar melodies to get a feel for the controls. The more you experiment, the more comfortable you'll become with your instrument.

- **Create and Innovate:** The Otamatone is a gateway to creativity, joy, and musical exploration. Embrace the whimsy and endless possibilities it offers. Start with basic tunes, familiar melodies, and simple compositions to build confidence. As you become more comfortable, let your creativity soar. Compose unique pieces, experiment with different genres, and let your imagination run wild.

With your Otamatone unboxed and assembled, you've taken the first steps on a delightful musical journey. The

Otamatone's unique design, easy assembly, and user-friendly interface make it accessible and enjoyable for musicians of all levels.

Armed with freshly installed batteries, a securely assembled Otamatone, and a basic understanding of its interface and controls, you're now ready to dive deeper. In the following chapters, you'll explore various playing techniques, methods for creating melodies, and innovative approaches to unlock the full potential of your Otamatone.

Chapter 3: Basic Playing Techniques

The Otamatone may look like a toy, but it's a full-fledged musical instrument with endless possibilities. To harness its magic, you must understand its various parts, learn how to position your hands correctly, and grasp the fundamentals of producing sound and controlling pitch. In this chapter, you'll dive headfirst into playing the Otamatone.

Whether you're a novice or have some musical experience under your belt, this chapter breaks down the essential techniques. From getting to know the different Otamatone parts to mastering proper hand positioning and finger technique, this chapter is your gateway to unlocking the melodic potential of this whimsical instrument.

Proper Hand Positioning and Finger Technique

To truly master this unique and charming instrument, you need more than enthusiasm. You need the right techniques. This section explores the essential aspects of proper hand positioning and finger technique on the Otamatone to take your melodies to the next level.

3. *Holding your Otamatone properly can take your melodies to the next level. Source: https://preview.redd.it/4lzlho9aahc91.png?width=596&format=png&auto=webp&s=55decd133a2193820d5217ea97be035b4cc4a61d*

The Heart of the Otamatone

Before learning hand positioning and finger technique, here's a quick recap of the fundamentals. This instrument comprises a stem-like body, a musical note head with a cheerful face, and a mouth interface, where the real magic happens. By sliding your fingers along the rubber strip on the stem, you control the pitch and produce a range of electronic tones, creating enchanting melodies bound to bring a smile to your face.

The Importance of Proper Hand Positioning

Proper hand positioning is essential for several reasons:

- **Precision:** To hit the right notes accurately, your fingers must be in the right place at the right time.

- **Comfort:** Correct hand positioning ensures you play for extended periods without discomfort or fatigue.

- **Expressiveness:** By mastering hand positioning, you gain control over the instrument's nuances and dynamics, allowing you to infuse your music with your emotions.

Basic Hand Position

For correct hand positioning, follow these steps:

1. **Support the Head:** Hold the Otamatone's head in your non-dominant hand. This hand provides support and stability for the instrument.

2. **Mouth Interface Access:** With your non-dominant hand holding the stem, your dominant hand will have easy access to the mouth interface.

3. **Finger Placement:** Place your dominant hand's fingers on the Otamatone's rubber strip. Keep your fingers relaxed, and let them rest lightly on the strip. You don't need to press hard to produce sounds.

4. **Vertical Position:** Keep your hand in a vertical position. Your fingers should be parallel to the rubber strip. Avoid angling your hand, as it may lead to unintentional pitch changes.

5. **Begin Playing:** With your hand in the correct position, slide your fingers up and down the strip to produce various notes. Practice becoming comfortable with different finger placements and the corresponding sounds they create.

Mastering Finger Technique

Proper hand positioning is the foundation, but your finger technique will add finesse to your music. Here's how to master it:

- **Finger Mobility:** Your fingers are tools for creating music. Practice moving them smoothly up and down the rubber strip. Keep your movements fluid, avoiding jerky or abrupt slides.

- **Pressure Control:** The pressure you apply to the rubber strip influences the note's intensity. Light pressure produces softer tones, while firm pressure creates louder and more pronounced notes. Experiment with different pressure levels for a full range of expressions.

- **Finger Spacing**: As you slide your fingers along the strip, you'll notice the spacing between them affects the pitch. Wider spacing between fingers generally results in lower notes, while closer spacing produces higher notes. To create intentional pitch changes, pay attention to finger spacing.

Troubleshooting Common Challenges

You may encounter some common challenges when you first start playing the Otamatone. Here are solutions for a few of them:

- **Unintentional Sounds:** If you're getting unintended notes while playing, make sure your hand positioning is correct and your fingers are not accidentally touching the rubber strip.

- **Inconsistent Volume**: If your volume varies greatly during your performance, practice controlling the pressure you apply to the rubber strip for consistent sound.

- **Pitch Jumps:** Sudden pitch jumps occur if your fingers aren't sliding smoothly. Focus on maintaining a consistent and even slide.

Let Your Creativity Flow

Remember, the Otamatone is a canvas for your musical creativity. With the right-hand positioning and finger technique, you'll express yourself and create melodies that resonate with your emotions and imagination. So, don't be afraid to explore, practice, and let your creativity flow. Whether playing catchy tunes, recreating classic melodies, or composing music, the Otamatone is your companion.

Produce Sounding and Controlling Pitch

With its playful appearance and unique sound, the Otamatone promises to delight and entertain. But how do you produce sound and control the pitch?

Mastering the Art of Sound Production

Playing the Otamatone isn't only about squeezing the stem and hoping for the best. It's also about mastering the art of sound production.

1. **The Power of Pressure:** To create sound on the Otamatone, apply gentle pressure to the rubber strip with your fingers. The pressure you exert directly affects the intensity of the notes you produce. You'll notice a soft, delicate sound as you lightly touch the strip and slide your fingers. Now, apply a bit more pressure, and you'll hear the

sound become louder and more pronounced. The key is to find the right balance.

2. **Fluid Sliding:** To produce smooth, consistent sounds, slide your fingers up and down the rubber strip with fluid motions. Avoid abrupt or jerky movements, as these will result in pitch fluctuations or unintended notes. Let your fingers dance along the strip, effortlessly creating your melodies.

The Fine Art of Pitch Control

Controlling pitch on the Otamatone is where the magic truly happens. The rubber strip's versatility is key to producing a wide range of notes and crafting enchanting melodies.

The Pitch Range

The Otamatone offers an impressive pitch range, allowing you to produce a variety of tones. You effortlessly switch from high-pitched, whimsical notes to deeper, mellow sounds by sliding your fingers along the rubber strip. This range makes the Otamatone very versatile, enabling you to create music across different genres and styles. Otamatones also have a switch on the back that cycles between octaves – low, medium, and high.

Mastering Pitch Control

To become a true Otamatone master, you must practice pitch control. Here are a few things to consider:

- **Sensitivity:** Develop sensitivity in your fingers. Your ability to apply varying pressure and control your finger spacing directly impacts the precision of your pitch control.

- **Ear Training**: Pay close attention to the sounds you're producing. Your ears are your best guide. Train your musical ear to recognize different pitches and their positions on the rubber strip.

- **Visual Aids:** Some Otamatones have markings on the rubber strip to indicate specific notes. These are valuable visual aids, especially for beginners. They help you identify and remember the various notes' positions.

- **Practice Scales:** Practicing scales is an excellent way to fine-tune pitch control. Start with simple scales and gradually work your way up to more complex ones. It will improve your skills and enhance your understanding of the Otamatone's pitch range.

Troubleshooting Pitch Challenges

As you embark on your Otamatone journey, you might encounter a few common pitch-related challenges. Here's how to troubleshoot two of the most common ones:

- **Pitch Inconsistencies:** If your notes unexpectedly vary in pitch, there might be issues with your finger control. Practice keeping your finger spacing and pressure consistent during your slides. Additionally, make sure your fingers make full contact with the rubber strip to avoid unintentional pitch changes.

- **Pitch Jumps**: Sudden jumps in pitch are disconcerting. It usually happens when you're not maintaining a steady and smooth slide. To overcome this, practice sliding your fingers with uniform pressure without interruptions in your movement.

Embrace the Learning Curve

Learning to produce sound and control pitch on the Otamatone is a fun and rewarding experience. Embrace the learning curve, and remember, practice is your greatest ally. Here are a few tips:

1. **Start Slow:** Begin with simple melodies at a slow pace. It will help you develop sound production and pitch basics without feeling overwhelmed.

2. **Experiment with Different Techniques:** Don't be afraid to explore various finger techniques, pressures, and spacings. The Otamatone rewards experimentation, so let your creativity shine.

3. **Record Yourself**: Recording your practice sessions will provide valuable feedback. It allows you to analyze your performance and track your progress over time.

4. **Play Along with Music**: Playing along with your favorite songs is a fantastic way to develop your sound production and pitch control skills.

The Otamatone is an invitation to create, explore, and delight in music. With the proper techniques for sound production and pitch control, you'll unlock the full potential of this whimsical instrument.

Chapter 4: Learning Otamatone Tones and Scales

The Otamatone's range of tones and scales is as diverse as a candy store, offering sweet, high-pitched notes and rich, flavorful low tones. It's a symphony of smiles and laughter, where you're the conductor, composer, and the audience.

In this chapter, you'll explore exciting music creation on the Otamatone. Whether you're a complete beginner or have some musical experience, understanding tones and scales is a pivotal step.

Otamatone's Scale and Pitch Range

The Otamatone has taken the music world by storm with its unique design and charming sound. But what is the Otamatone's scale and pitch range, and how can you unlock its full potential?

4. Understanding an Otamatone's scale and pitch range can help you play it better. Source: Ofeky, Attribution, via Wikimedia Commons: https://commons.wikimedia.org/wiki/File:Music_note_A.jpg

The Musical Spectrum

The Otamatone boasts an impressive pitch range, giving you the power to create an array of sounds. The Otamatone's musical spectrum is bound to captivate your ears and heart, from high-pitched, whimsical notes that seem to dance with joy to deeper, mellower tones that resonate with warmth.

1. **High Notes:** At the higher end of the pitch range, the Otamatone produces delightful, cheerful notes that sound like giggles frozen in mid-air. These high-pitched tones add a whimsical touch to your melodies and are perfect for creating playful, light-hearted compositions. Imagine a joyful conversation with birds in the treetops or a chorus of laughter from a room full of delighted children.

2. **Mid-Range Tones:** The mid-range of the Otamatone's pitch scale is the heart of your melodies. These notes are versatile and can adapt to a variety of musical styles. Here, you will craft beautiful, lyrical tunes expressing a wide range of emotions. You'll find the joy of painting a canvas with an extensive palette of colors, each note offering a unique shade of sound to your musical masterpiece.

3. **Low Notes:** As you descend into the lower notes of the Otamatone's scale, you'll discover a sense of resonance and depth that adds a rich texture to your music. These help you mimic the rumbling of distant thunder or the soothing purr of a contented cat. They provide a strong foundation for your compositions, making them more profound and moving.

With the Otamatone's enchanting scale and pitch range at your disposal, you're ready for a musical adventure like no other. Whether composing imaginative tunes, recreating classic melodies, or experimenting with unique sounds, the Otamatone invites you to explore and create. Its versatile range allows you to dabble in various genres, from joyful playfulness to heartfelt ballads.

Memorizing and Practicing Basic Notes and Scales

Understanding basic notes and scales is the foundation of playing any musical instrument. The Otamatone is no exception. The following explores the basic notes and scales of the Otamatone.

The Musical Alphabet

Before you dive into scales and melodies, you must start with the musical alphabet. In Western music, letters (A, B, C, D, E, F, G) represent different notes. These notes are the building blocks of music, and understanding them is crucial for playing any instrument, including the Otamatone.

Here's a quick rundown of the musical alphabet:

1. A: The starting point of the musical alphabet. It's the note that sets the stage for the entire musical piece.

2. B: The next note in the alphabet. It follows A and precedes C.

3. C: A significant musical note, often serving as a reference point for scales. It's immediately followed by D.

4. D: The fourth note in the sequence.

5. E: The fifth note and follows D.

6. F: A step higher than E.

7. G: The final note in the musical alphabet, ending the sequence.

These seven notes are the foundation of most Western music and what you'll use to play your Otamatone.

Understanding Scales

In music, scales are a series of notes played in ascending or descending order. They are the basis for melodies, harmonies, and chords. One of the most common scales is the major scale. It's often used in cheerful, upbeat melodies and has a recognizable sound.

The C major scale comprises the notes C, D, E, F, G, A, B and C. When played in sequence, it creates a distinct musical pattern. Other scales, like the minor scale, have their unique sequences of notes, producing different emotional qualities in music.

Memorizing Notes and Scales

After you've had a taste of playing a basic scale, it's time to talk about memorizing notes and scales on your

Otamatone. Here are tips to help you commit them to memory:

- **Visual Aids:** Consider creating a visual reference. You can draw or print a simple diagram of the Otamatone's rubber strip with notes labeled. It will be a quick reference when you play.

- **Repetition:** Repetition is the mother of skill. The more you play scales and melodies, the more familiar you become with the note positions on the strip.

- **Use Mnemonics:** Create mnemonic devices or catchy phrases to help you remember the note sequences. For instance, remember the C major scale as "Do, Re, Mi, Fa, So, La, Ti, Do."

- **Practice with Intervals:** Practice playing intervals once you've memorized the C major scale. An interval is the distance between two notes. Try playing different combinations of notes to understand how intervals work and develop your sense of melody.

- **Learn One Scale at a Time:** Don't become overwhelmed by trying to learn multiple scales at once. Start with the C major scale, and once you're comfortable, move on to other scales, like the G major scale or the A minor scale.

- **Online Resources:** Take advantage of online resources and tutorials. You will find videos and diagrams showing where to place your fingers for various scales and melodies on the Otamatone.

As you immerse yourself in the Otamatone and master the art of notes and scales, don't forget to savor the joy of playing. The Otamatone is a delightful instrument that invites creativity and playfulness. You'll memorize notes and scales with practice and develop a deep connection with the instrument.

So, pick up your Otamatone, start with the C major scale, and explore the possibilities. Whether playing a well-known melody or creating compositions, the Otamatone is your tool for musical expression.

Developing Finger Dexterity for Smooth Transitions

In this section, you'll explore finger dexterity and how it leads to smooth transitions on the Otamatone.

The Role of Finger Dexterity

Finger dexterity refers to the skill and flexibility of your fingers in controlling the instrument. On the Otamatone, this skill is crucial because smooth transitions between notes and pitches are at the heart of creating beautiful melodies. Whether playing a classic tune, a modern hit or composing your own music, finger dexterity is indispensable.

5. Finger dexterity plays a crucial role when playing the Otamatone. Source: https://www.pexels.com/photo/person-s-hand-in-shallow-photo-1454797/

Why Smooth Transitions Matter

Smooth transitions between notes and pitches are essential for several reasons:

- **Musicality:** Smooth transitions enhance the overall musicality of your performance. It allows your music to flow seamlessly, captivating your audience.

- **Expressiveness:** Fluid transitions enable you to express yourself with more subtlety. You control the dynamics and emotions of your performance.

- **Complex Melodies**: If you aspire to play complex melodies or compositions, smooth transitions are necessary. They prevent your music from sounding choppy or disjointed.

- **Creative Freedom:** With finger dexterity, you gain the freedom to explore and experiment with your music. You will push the boundaries of your creativity.

Exercises for Developing Finger Dexterity

Here are fun and effective exercises to help you develop finger dexterity on your Otamatone:

- **Scales and Arpeggios**: Like with a traditional instrument, practicing scales and arpeggios (when the notes of a chord are played in rapid succession) will significantly improve finger dexterity. Start with simple scales and gradually work up to more complex ones.

- **Chromatic Exercises**: Play a series of chromatic notes (notes that don't belong to the scale in which the harmony is written), ascending or descending, to challenge your fingers' flexibility. These exercises will help you improve finger independence and agility.

- **Interval Jumps:** Work on playing notes not adjacent to each other. For example, try jumping from a lower note to one several steps higher. This exercise will train your fingers to make larger transitions smoothly.

- **Staccato and Legato:** Alternate between staccato (short, detached notes) and legato (smooth, connected notes). It will help you control the articulation of your music, making it more expressive.

- **Scale Variations:** Practice scales with different finger patterns. For instance, you can use your thumb and index finger for ascending scales and your middle and ring fingers for descending scales. This exercise enhances your finger independence.

Tips for Improving Finger Dexterity

In addition to these exercises, here are tips to enhance your finger dexterity:

- **Practice Regularly:** Consistency is key. Dedicate time each day to practice your finger exercises. Regular practice will gradually improve your finger dexterity.

- **Start Slow:** When trying new exercises, start at a slow tempo. As you become more comfortable, gradually increase the speed. You have to maintain control even when playing fast.

- **Focus on Precision:** Pay attention to hitting the right notes accurately. Precision is the cornerstone of smooth transitions.

- **Use a Metronome:** A metronome will help you maintain a steady tempo while practicing. It's an excellent tool for building finger dexterity and rhythm.

- **Experiment and Challenge Yourself:** Don't be afraid to try new exercises and techniques. Challenge yourself with different musical styles and genres to expand your musical horizons.

- **Record Your Practice Sessions:** Recording your practice sessions can be incredibly valuable. It allows you to review your performance, identify areas for improvement, and track your progress.

Common Challenges and Solutions

You may face common challenges as you develop finger dexterity for smooth transitions. Here are solutions to a few:

- **Inaccurate Notes:** If you struggle with accuracy, slow down. Take your time to hit the right notes. Speed will come with practice.

- **Stiff Fingers:** Stiff fingers will hinder transitions. Make sure your fingers are relaxed and nimble. Stretch them before practice to improve flexibility.

- **Uneven Playing:** Uneven playing results from uneven pressure on the Otamatone's strip. Practice controlling the pressure to maintain a consistent sound.

- **Lack of Independence:** Practicing finger independence exercises will help them loosen up if they feel "glued" together. Train each finger to move independently to allow smoother transitions.

Remember, developing finger dexterity is not only about reaching a goal. It's about enjoying the process. The Otamatone is a unique and playful instrument, and the journey of improving your finger dexterity should be just as fun. The key to mastering finger dexterity is practice, patience, and a passion for music. Embrace the learning curve, make music that makes you smile, and celebrate every small victory along the way.

So, keep playing, keep learning, and keep those melodies flowing. As you find your flow, you'll discover a world of musical possibilities where smooth transitions and captivating melodies become second nature.

Chapter 5: Playing Your First Melodies and Songs

Playing your first melodies and songs on the Otamatone is a magical experience. You'll be transported to a world of musical delight from the moment you press your fingers on the rubber strip and create electronic tones. As you practice, you'll feel a sense of accomplishment with each note you master. The Otamatone's unique design and the knowledge you've acquired will soon have you composing melodies, adding your personal touch to this enchanting instrument.

6. *Practicing will lead you to feel a sense of accomplishment with each note you master. Source: https://pixabay.com/photos/music-sheet-in-a-shadow-flute-piano-5117328/*

In this chapter, you'll discover playing your first melodies and songs. Your newfound knowledge will transform into beautiful music, evoking emotions and sparking your creative spirit. You've come a long way. Now, it's time to apply your fingerings and techniques to create melodic magic, explore basic music notation and rhythm, and play beginner-friendly tunes to build confidence as a budding Otamatone player.

Applying Fingerings and Techniques to Play Melodies

Now that you're familiar with the basic hand positioning and finger technique, it's time to put them to use. Playing melodies on the Otamatone involves sliding your fingers along the rubber strip to produce different notes. Here's how you can apply your fingerings and techniques effectively:

1. **Start with Simple Tunes:** As a beginner, it's a good idea to begin with simple melodies. Songs like "Mary Had a Little Lamb" or "Jingle Bells" are excellent choices. These tunes consist of a limited range of notes and provide a perfect platform to practice finger movements and pitch control.

2. **Experiment with Sliding:** The unique characteristic of the Otamatone lies in its sliding mechanism. Experiment with various sliding techniques to create varying pitches and explore the instrument's vocal-like qualities. Remember, keep your fingers relaxed to maintain a smooth, controlled glide along the rubber strip.

3. **Mastering the Note Selector:** The note selector at the top of your Otamatone's head is where you

choose your desired pitch. It's essential to become comfortable with changing the notes as you play. Practice sliding your fingers to different positions and stopping at specific notes to get a feel for the instrument's range.

4. **Play Along with Familiar Songs**: One of the best ways to apply your fingerings and techniques is to play along with songs you know and love. Use online resources or sheet music of your favorite tunes to guide your practice. It adds an element of familiarity and fun to your learning process.

5. **Create Your Melodies:** Don't hesitate to let your creativity flow. Compose your melodies and experiment with different note combinations. The Otamatone is a canvas for musical ideas and your chance to let your imagination run wild.

Introduction to Basic Music Notation and Rhythm

While playing the Otamatone is primarily about having fun, a basic understanding of music notation and rhythm will elevate your playing. These concepts provide structure and help you interpret music more effectively. Here's a brief introduction to get you started:

- **Musical Notation:** Music notation is a written language for music. It uses symbols to represent notes, rhythms, and other musical elements. While it might seem complex initially, understanding the basics will greatly assist your learning process. Start by familiarizing yourself with note names, like whole notes, half notes, and quarter notes.

Learn how to read simple sheet music so you can easily follow along with your favorite songs.

- **Rhythm:** Rhythm is the heartbeat of music. It's the timing and pattern of sounds and silences. You will enhance your rhythmic skills by practicing with a metronome. A metronome helps you maintain a steady tempo while playing. Start with simple rhythms and gradually progress to more complex patterns.

- **Timing and Counting**: When reading sheet music, timing is crucial. You'll often see time signatures like 4/4 or 3/4, indicating the number of beats in a measure. Learning to count beats and understanding how long notes are held is essential for playing in time and maintaining rhythm.

- **Musical Phrasing**: Phrasing shapes a musical passage by emphasizing certain notes or groups of notes. It adds dynamics and expressiveness to your playing. Listen to how experienced Otamatone players interpret the music's phrasing, and try to replicate those nuances in your performances.

Playing Beginner-Friendly Tunes to Build Confidence

Building confidence is essential as you play your first melodies and songs on the Otamatone. Starting with beginner-friendly tunes is an excellent way to ease into music. Here are well-loved songs perfect for beginners:

- **"Ode to Joy" by Beethoven:** This classical piece is simple for beginners. Its melody is instantly recognizable and a joy to play on the Otamatone.

- **"Twinkle, Twinkle, Little Star":** A childhood favorite, usually this tune is one of the first songs learned as kids and a great starting point for novice Otamatone players.

- **"You Are My Sunshine":** With its heartwarming lyrics and melody, this song is a delightful choice for beginners. Its slow tempo allows you to focus on your fingerings and technique.

- **"Hedwig's Theme" from Harry Potter:** If you're a fan of the wizarding world, you'll love playing this melody. Its simplicity makes it accessible for beginners.

- **"Happy Birthday":** A classic celebratory tune, playing "Happy Birthday" on your Otamatone is a delightful way to mark special occasions and showcase your progress.

- **"Auld Lang Syne":** This traditional folk song is commonly played on New Year's Eve. Its memorable melody and slow tempo make it a wonderful choice for beginners to practice their finger dexterity.

Tips for Playing Your First Melodies and Songs

As you play your first melodies and songs on the Otamatone, here are a few helpful tips:

- **Take It One Step at a Time:** Learning to play the Otamatone is a gradual process. Don't rush. Take it one step at a time. Focus on one song or melody until you feel comfortable before moving on to the next.

- **Listen Actively:** Pay attention to how experienced players interpret the music. Listen to their phrasing, dynamics, and nuances. It will help you understand the emotional aspect of playing.

- **Record Your Performances**: Recording your practice sessions and performances is incredibly beneficial. It allows you to evaluate your progress, identify areas for improvement, and see how far you've come.

- **Practice Regularly:** Consistent practice is vital to improvement. Dedicate time each day to practice, even for a short while. It's the cumulative effect of practice that leads to growth.

- **Have Fun:** Remember, playing the Otamatone is about having fun. Enjoy the process, and don't be too hard on yourself.

Playing your first melodies and songs on the Otamatone is a remarkable milestone in your musical journey. It's the moment when the instrument truly comes alive. As you practice your fingerings and techniques, delve into basic music notation and rhythm, and play beginner-friendly songs to build confidence, you'll fall in love with the magic of the Otamatone.

Embrace this chapter of your musical journey with open arms. Celebrate each note you master, each song you play, and each melody you create. Whether playing for yourself, friends, or an audience, the joy of making music on the Otamatone is an experience unequaled. So, keep practicing, keep playing, and keep letting your melodies fill the world with happiness and wonder. Your journey has only just begun, and the musical adventures that lie ahead are bound to be extraordinary.

Chapter 6: Adding Expression and Effects

Using expression and effects with your Otamatone playing adds color to the blank canvas, transforming it into a vibrant masterpiece. It's when your melodies become a tapestry of emotions and creativity. With techniques for varying dynamics and volume, the introduction of expressive techniques like vibrato, and the exploration of effects, you have the power to craft music that captivates hearts and ignites the imagination.

7. *Certain techniques will help you become more expressive with the Otamatone. Source:*
https://www.flickr.com/photos/yto/4294598621/in/photostream/

Whether you want to add a touch of elegance with vibrato, create echoes with delay, or experiment with distortion for a rock-inspired sound, the Otamatone becomes a versatile tool for self-expression and musical innovation.

You've learned the fundamentals, mastered hand positioning, and played your first melodies. Now, it's time to take your musical adventure to the next level by adding expression and effects to your performances. This chapter is about elevating your playing and infusing your music with emotion and creativity. It's time to enter the captivating world of effects and expression on the Otamatone.

Techniques for Varying Dynamics and Volume

Expression in music is the art of infusing your performance with emotions and dynamics. On the Otamatone, varying dynamics and volume are essential for conveying moods and intensities in your melodies. Here are techniques to help you:

- **Pressure Control**: One of the most fundamental ways to vary dynamics on the Otamatone is by controlling the applied pressure to the rubber strip. Light pressure produces softer, more delicate notes, while firm pressure creates louder and more pronounced ones. Experiment with different degrees of pressure to understand the full range of dynamics at your disposal.

- **Consistent Sliding:** Smooth and consistent sliding along the rubber strip also affects dynamics. Gradually sliding your finger up and down creates a crescendo or decrescendo effect. The key is to maintain control and precision while transitioning between notes.

- **Combining Finger Movements:** Consider combining different finger movements to add depth and complexity to your melodies. For instance, start softly with one finger and introduce more fingers or firmer pressure as the melody progresses. This technique allows you to craft dynamic and expressive performances.

- **Staccato and Legato:** Altering between staccato (short, detached notes) and legato (smooth, connected notes) is a fantastic way to add expression. Experiment with these techniques to create a contrast between sharp, percussive notes and smooth, flowing passages.

Introduction to Vibrato and Other Expressive Techniques

Vibrato is a beautiful and expressive technique that adds a touch of elegance and emotion to your playing. It's characterized by a rapid, slight variation in pitch, creating a shimmering effect. While the traditional vibrato technique in classical music may not directly apply to the Otamatone, you can create a similar effect by gently wobbling your finger on the rubber strip while maintaining a consistent airflow. This subtle oscillation of pitch adds a layer of expressiveness to your melodies.

In addition to vibrato, here are other expressive techniques you can explore:

- **Glissando:** A glissando is a sliding technique, rapidly moving your finger up or down the rubber strip to create a sweeping effect. It's perfect for conveying movement and rising anticipation.

- **Tremolo:** Tremolo is achieved by rapidly alternating between two or more notes. This technique adds intensity and excitement to your melodies. Experiment with different note combinations to find the tremolo pattern that suits your music.

- **Pitch Bending:** Gently bending the rubber strip with your fingers produces a subtle pitch bend effect. It's an expressive technique often used in contemporary and electronic music.

- **Muting:** By placing your fingers gently on the rubber strip without sliding, you create a muted or percussive effect. This technique is particularly useful for adding rhythmic elements to your performances.

Exploring Using Effects to Enhance Your Playing

Effects add an extra layer of creativity and intrigue to your Otamatone performances. While the instrument can produce a unique and whimsical sound, you can enhance it even more by using external effects. Here are some effects you can explore:

- **Reverb**: Reverb adds spaciousness and depth to your sound. It simulates the sound reflection off walls, creating a more immersive auditory experience. You can achieve this effect by connecting your Otamatone to a reverb pedal or using digital effects processors.

- **Delay**: Delay is the repetition of a sound after a short period. It creates echoes and a sense of space in your music. Using a delay effect is particularly effective in Otamatone solos and ambient compositions.

- **Distortion**: Distortion adds grit and crunch to your sound, transforming it into something edgier. It's perfect for creating rock or experimental music with the Otamatone. Connect your instrument to a distortion pedal or a guitar amplifier to add distortion.

- **Chorus:** Chorus produces a shimmering, swirling effect by slightly detuning and delaying the original sound. It's great for adding a dreamy quality to your music. A chorus pedal will achieve this effect.

- **Pitch Shifting**: Pitch shifting allows you to change the pitch of your Otamatone's sound. This effect creates harmonies, layers melodies, or produces unique textures in your compositions.

Tips for Adding Expression and Effects

As you venture into adding expression and effects to your Otamatone playing, here are tips to guide you:

- **Listen and Learn:** Listen to professional musicians and experienced Otamatone players. Pay attention to how they use expression and effects in their music. You will gain valuable insights and inspiration from their performances.

- **Experiment and Explore:** Don't be afraid to experiment with different effects and expressive techniques. It's through experimentation that you'll discover your unique style and sound.

- **Start Simple:** When using effects, start with simple settings and gradually explore more complex ones. It allows you to understand how each effect influences your sound.

- **Practice and Patience:** Like any aspect of playing an instrument, adding expression and effects requires practice and patience. Keep refining your skills, and don't get discouraged by initial challenges.

- **Record Your Performances**: Recording your practice sessions and performances is excellent for evaluating how expression and effects impact your music. It enables you to refine your techniques over time.

The Otamatone is a canvas for your musical creativity. By adding expression and effects to your playing, you transform its whimsical sounds into something truly remarkable. Whether creating emotive melodies, experimenting with effects, or infusing your music with expressive techniques, this chapter opens a world of musical possibilities.

Embrace the power of expression and effects on the Otamatone, and let your imagination soar. Whether playing for yourself, your friends, or a global audience, your unique sound and style will shine through. Your musical journey has reached a new and exciting phase.

Chapter 7: Exploring Creative Otamatone Techniques

In this chapter, you'll discover the fascinating world of creative Otamatone techniques. You've already learned the basics and mastered the essentials. Now it's time to push the boundaries, explore unconventional methods, experiment with the Otamatone's unique sound, and incorporate creativity into your playing style.

8. Be creative when experimenting with the Otamatone's unique sound. Source: https://www.pexels.com/photo/close-up-of-human-hand-256514/

Introduction to Unconventional Techniques

The Otamatone is not your typical instrument and certainly doesn't limit you to conventional playing methods. It's a canvas for experimentation, and this section introduces you to unconventional techniques that will redefine how you play the Otamatone. Here are creative techniques to get you started:

- **Slides:** Sliding your finger along the rubber strip is one of the core techniques, but you can take it a step further. Experiment with long, sweeping slides that span the entire range of the Otamatone. This technique creates a captivating, dreamy effect perfect for ethereal melodies.

- **Glissandos**: A glissando involves rapidly moving your finger up and down the rubber strip. This technique produces a dazzling and dynamic effect that will add drama and excitement to your music. Imagine a cascade of notes making your melodies come alive.

- **Percussive Tapping**: Don't limit yourself to sliding. Try tapping your fingers on the rubber strip to create percussive effects. It's a technique that infuses rhythmic elements into your playing and makes your music more engaging.

- **Harmonics:** Like a guitar, the Otamatone has harmonic points where you can lightly touch the rubber strip to produce subtle, bell-like tones. Experiment with harmonics to add a unique sparkle to your melodies.

Using the Otamatone's Unique Sound for Experimental Music

The Otamatone's unique sound is a treasure trove for experimental music enthusiasts. It's unlike any other instrument, and its quirky, electronic tones can create avant-garde compositions and soundscapes. Here's how you can use the Otamatone for experimental music:

- **Layering and Looping:** Create complex soundscapes by layering different melodies and loops. The Otamatone's playful sound makes it an ideal instrument for building intricate textures and patterns.

- **Sound Effects and Manipulation:** Experiment with sound effects processors to modify and shape the sound. Effects like delay, reverb, and distortion will take your experimental music to new dimensions.

- **Collaboration**: Join other musicians with different instruments to experiment with varying sounds and combinations.

- **Soundscapes and Ambience:** Use the Otamatone to create ambient soundscapes. Its whimsical tones evoke dreamy atmospheres and is an excellent tool for setting moods and emotions in experimental compositions.

Incorporating Your Creativity into Your Playing Style

This section is about empowering you to incorporate your unique creativity into your playing style. Here are tips to help you infuse your music with your personal touch:

- **Composing Original Music:** Don't limit yourself to playing existing songs. Compose your music, whether a catchy melody, an emotive ballad, or an experimental masterpiece. Let your imagination run wild and create something entirely your own.

- **Storytelling Through Music:** Music has the power to tell stories and convey emotions. Use your Otamatone to create musical narratives that transport your audience to different worlds, evoke powerful emotions, and leave a lasting impact.

- **Embracing Mistakes**: Not every note has to be perfect. Embrace the imperfections and occasional "mistakes." They can lead to unexpected, creative discoveries and add character to your music.

- **Exploring Different Genres:** The Otamatone is versatile and can adapt to various musical genres. Don't hesitate to explore different styles, from classical to rock to electronic. Each genre offers unique opportunities for creative expression.

- **Recording and Sharing**: Record your performances and compositions to share with the world. Platforms like YouTube and SoundCloud are fantastic for showcasing your creativity and connecting with a global audience of music enthusiasts.

Tips for Exploring Creative Otamatone Techniques

As you embark on your journey to explore creative Otamatone techniques, here are tips to guide you:

- **Be Humble:** Experimenting with unconventional techniques and experimental music can be overwhelming. Start with simple ideas and gradually build complexity into your playing.

- **Learn from Others**: Listen to other musicians, Otamatone players, and those from different musical backgrounds. You will gain inspiration and insights from a wide range of sources.

- **Take Breaks:** Creativity thrives when you give your mind time to rest and rejuvenate. Don't be afraid to step away from your instrument and return with a fresh perspective.

- **Feedback and Collaboration:** Seek feedback from fellow musicians and collaborators. Collaboration introduces you to new techniques and broadens your creative horizons.

- **Stay Open-Minded:** Embrace the unexpected. Some of the most innovative and groundbreaking music has been born from a willingness to step outside the comfort zone.

You'll discover a world of musical possibilities as you explore unconventional techniques, experiment with the instrument's unique sound, and incorporate your boundless creativity into your playing. Your Otamatone becomes a vessel for your imagination, and the music you create reflects your unique style and personality.

Embrace the unexpected, let your ideas soar, and never underestimate the creative potential of this instrument. The journey ahead is one of innovation and discovery, and the music you'll create is bound to be remarkable.

Chapter 8: Progressing as an Otamatone Player

In this final chapter, you'll discover the secrets of progressing as an Otamatone player. This isn't just a conclusion but a doorway to endless possibilities and musical adventures. So, dive in and discover how you can continue evolving, learning, and improving.

Setting Personal Goals and Tracking Your Progress

9. Set goals for your development as an Otamatone player. Source: https://www.pexels.com/photo/green-typewriter-on-brown-wooden-table-4052198/

The path to mastery begins with a clear vision. Setting personal goals allows you to define your musical aspirations and work toward achieving them. Start by identifying specific skills you want to improve, songs you aim to play, or creative projects you wish to undertake. These goals are your roadmap, guiding your practice sessions and motivating you to push your boundaries. Don't forget to track your progress diligently. Whether mastering a challenging melody, refining your technique, or composing an original piece, keeping a record of your achievements provides a tangible sense of accomplishment, inspiring you to reach even greater heights.

Exploring More Advanced Melodies and Creative Projects

Now that you have a solid foundation, it's time to explore more advanced melodies and creative projects. Challenge yourself with intricate tunes from diverse genres, spanning classical compositions to contemporary hits. Analyze these melodies, dissecting them into manageable segments to enhance your understanding. Also, consider composing your own music. Experiment with different chord progressions, rhythms, and melodies. Your Otamatone will be a canvas for innovation, enabling you to craft original compositions reflecting your unique style and musical voice.

Seek Inspiration from Other Otamatone Players and Resources

One of the most powerful sources of inspiration is the community of Otamatone players and the wealth of resources available. Engage with fellow enthusiasts, sharing experiences, tips, and challenges. Online forums, social media groups, and Otamatone-focused communities provide platforms to connect with players from various skill levels, opening avenues for collaborative projects and shared learning. Additionally, immerse yourself in the works of seasoned Otamatone artists. Watch their performances, dissect their techniques, and draw inspiration from their creativity. Learning from others expands your skill set and ignites fresh ideas.

Tips for Continuous Improvement and Expanding Your Skills

Continuous improvement is the cornerstone of mastery. Here are tips to facilitate your growth as an Otamatone player:

- **Consistent Practice**: Dedicate regular, focused practice sessions to refine your skills. Establish a practice routine accommodating your schedule and adhering to your goals. Consistency is crucial for improvement.

- **Feedback and Evaluation**: Seek feedback from experienced musicians, teachers, or fellow players. Constructive criticism provides valuable insights, highlighting areas for improvement that might have gone unnoticed. Embrace feedback as a catalyst for growth.

- **Explore Music Theory**: Understanding music theory enhances your ability to interpret melodies, improvise, and compose. Familiarize yourself with key concepts like scales, chords, and rhythm.

Online tutorials and music theory books tailored for beginners simplify complex topics.

- **Ear Training:** Developing your hearing allows you to play by ear, grasp melodies intuitively, and enhance your improvisational skills. Engage in ear training exercises to recognize intervals, chords, and progressions. Numerous online tools and apps offer interactive ear training modules.

- **Experiment with Different Genres:** Embrace versatility by exploring various musical genres. Each genre introduces unique techniques, styles, and challenges. From classical and jazz to pop and electronic music, diversifying your repertoire broadens your musical horizons.

- **Embrace Technology:** Leverage technology to enhance your playing. Use apps and software with virtual instruments, metronomes, tuners, and recording capabilities. These tools aid in practicing, tuning, and capturing your musical ideas.

- **Attend Workshops and Classes:** Participate in Otamatone workshops, classes, and online tutorials. Engaging with skilled instructors provides personalized guidance, addressing specific challenges and refining your techniques. Workshops also facilitate networking with other players, fostering a supportive community.

- **Stay Inspired:** Cultivate a mindset of curiosity and wonder. Attend concerts, watch musical documentaries, and explore the rich history of music. Often, inspiration comes from unexpected sources, sparking creativity and fueling your passion for the Otamatone.

Resources for Ongoing Learning and Inspiration

To aid your ongoing learning and inspiration, here are valuable resources tailored for Otamatone enthusiasts:

10. Stay inspired by looking for different resources to help you learn more. Source:
https://www.flickr.com/photos/arselectronica/14663879989

- **Online Tutorials and YouTube Channels:** Explore   YouTube   channels   dedicated   to

Otamatone tutorials. One notable YouTube channel is "Maywa Denki," known for its quirky and creative Otamatone performances and tutorials. They provide valuable insights and techniques for beginners and experienced players.

- **Music Sheets and Tabs:** Numerous websites provide free and paid Otamatone music sheets and tabs. "Musescore" and "Sheet Music Plus" offer a wide range of Otamatone music sheets covering various genres and difficulty levels, enabling you to explore diverse melodies.

- **Online Communities:** Join online communities, forums, and social media groups centered on the Otamatone. The "r/Otamatone" subreddit on Reddit is a vibrant community of Otamatone enthusiasts, fostering collaborations, knowledge sharing, and mutual support. The Otamatone Discord server is a valuable hub for discussions, sharing resources, and connecting with players worldwide.

- **Music Theory Apps:** For music theory and ear training, "Music Theory Pro" and "Perfect Ear" are popular apps available for Android and iOS devices. These apps offer interactive lessons, quizzes, and exercises, enhancing your understanding of fundamental concepts.

- **Music Composition Software:** Experiment with music composition software and digital audio workstations (DAWs) like "GarageBand" (for Mac and iOS) and "FL Studio" (for Windows and macOS). These tools allow you to compose, arrange, and produce your music, providing a creative outlet for your musical ideas.

- **Live Performances and Concerts:** To watch live Otamatone performances and concerts featuring skilled players, watch for events hosted by the creators of Otamatone, "Maywa Denki." They occasionally perform live and showcase the instrument's potential in musical and comedic contexts.

- **Music Education Platforms:** Enroll in online music education platforms that offer courses tailored for Otamatone players. While specific courses on the Otamatone may be limited, platforms like Udemy and Skillshare provide music theory and composition courses beneficial for all musicians, including Otamatone enthusiasts.

As you embark on the journey of progressing as an Otamatone player, remember learning never ends. It merely transforms into new horizons and exciting challenges. Embrace each discovery, celebrate your achievements, and embrace the joy of continuous learning. Your dedication, creativity, and passion for the Otamatone will propel you toward unparalleled musical heights.

With your goals set, your techniques refined, and your inspiration kindled, the world of music opens its arms to welcome your unique voice. As you navigate the boundless realms of melodies, harmonies, and rhythms, your Otamatone becomes more than an instrument. It's an extension of your creative soul. So, venture forth, explore fearlessly, and let the melodies you create echo the beauty of your musical spirit.

Conclusion

Congratulations on completing your journey through "How to Play the Otamatone." You've embarked on a whimsical adventure, exploring the unique and delightful world of this peculiar yet enchanting musical instrument. Take a moment to recap what you've learned and reflect on the key takeaways that will guide your future endeavors with the Otamatone.

Key Takeaways

As you conclude your journey, here are the key takeaways to carry with you as you continue to play and explore the world of the Otamatone:

- **Uniqueness and Whimsy:** The Otamatone is more than an instrument. It's a unique and whimsical experience. Embrace its quirky nature and let your creativity shine through in every note.

- **Mastering the Basics:** A strong foundation is essential. From proper assembly and finger techniques to understanding notes and scales, mastering the basics is your stepping stone to musical proficiency.

- **Musical Notation and Melodies:** Delving into musical notation, scales, and melodies empowers you to play a vast range of music. The ability to read and interpret music opens doors to new melodies and compositions.

- **Expression and Creativity:** Don't limit yourself to notes and rhythms. Embrace expression, dynamics, and effects to infuse your performances with emotion and creativity. The Otamatone is a canvas for artistic expression.

- **Creative Exploration:** The Otamatone thrives on experimentation. Dive into unconventional techniques, compose original music, and collaborate with fellow musicians. Creativity knows no bounds.

- **Progress is a Journey**: Your musical journey is ongoing. Set goals, track your progress, and keep learning. Every note you play brings you closer to becoming a skilled Otamatone player.

- **Continuous Learning and Inspiration:** Seek inspiration from various sources, including fellow Otamatone players, resources, and educational platforms. Never stop exploring and expanding your musical horizons.

- **Community and Collaboration**: Connect with the global community of Otamatone enthusiasts. Collaborations, sharing experiences, and learning from one another are valuable aspects of your musical journey.

- **Technology and Innovation:** Embrace technology to enhance your playing. Use apps and digital tools for practice, composition, and recording, expanding your creative possibilities.

- **Diversify Your Repertoire:** Don't confine yourself to a single genre. The Otamatone is versatile, and exploring various musical styles broadens your musical horizons and keeps your journey exciting.

- **Celebrate Your Unique Voice:** Your playing style reflects your creativity and personality. Celebrate your unique voice and let it shine in every note you play on the Otamatone.

This book has equipped you with the skills to embark on a remarkable musical journey and hopefully ignited your passion for the Otamatone. Your feedback is invaluable, and hearing about your experiences and the music you create will help refine future editions. Please consider leaving a review to share your thoughts with others if you found this book helpful. Your journey as an Otamatone player is only beginning, and the possibilities are endless.

References

Easy ways to play an Otamatone: 13 steps (with pictures). (2019a, November 27). wikiHow. https://www.wikihow.com/Play-an-Otamatone

Easy ways to play an Otamatone: 13 steps (with pictures). (2019b, November 27). wikiHow. https://www.wikihow.com/Play-an-Otamatone

Hamee, U. S. (2020, November 24). Blogs: Learn songs for the Otamatone! Hamee.com - Hamee US. https://hamee.com/blogs/hamee-media/otamatone-notes-songs

Hamee, U. S. (2023, February 6). What is an Otamatone and the best way to enjoy it. Hamee.com - Hamee US. https://hamee.com/blogs/hamee-media/what-is-an-otamatone-and-the-best-way-to-enjoy-it

Learn to play the otamatone. (n.d.). Everythingotamatone.com. https://everythingotamatone.com/learn-to-play-the-otamatone/

Malmlund, M. (2021, April 10). Otamatone: Everything you need to know. Heavy. https://heavy.com/toys/otamatone-instrument/

Nakata, D. (2020, November 24). How to play Otamatone. Hamee.com - Hamee US. https://hamee.com/blogs/hamee-media/otamatone-how-to-play-otamatone

Ponthieux, T. (2023, February 13). A guide to Otamatone. Sugoi Mart by Japan Crate; Sugoi Mart by Japan Crate. https://sugoimart.com/blogs/sugoi-mart-blog/a-guide-to-otamatone

Reddit - dive into anything. (n.d.). Reddit.com.
https://www.reddit.com/r/Otamatone/comments/vs25b5/have_questio
ns_about_otamatones_start_here/

Standard. (n.d.). Everythingotamatone.com.
https://everythingotamatone.com/standard/

Zhou, D. [@mentalflow]. (2022, February 27). How to play otamatone: 4
tips for beginners. Youtube.
https://www.youtube.com/watch?v=ooPU6IkXjvk

Made in the USA
Las Vegas, NV
23 December 2024

15208321R00046